Jameelah Gets Dressed

Mini Mu'min Du'a Series #8

www.Mini-Mumin.com

Copyright © 2012 Mini Mu'min Publications

All rights reserved. This publication may not be reproduced in whole or in part by any means whatsoever without written permission from the copyright owner.

Introduction

All praise is due to Allah the Most High, may Allah send His blessings on the Prophet Muhammad (saw), his family, his companions, and those who follow him in righteousness until the Day of Judgment.

"And remember your Lord by your tongue and within yourself, humbly and in awe, without loudness, by words in the morning and the afternoon, and be not among those who are neglectful." (Holy Qur'an 7:205)

The **Mini Mu'min Du'a Series** is designed to help you teach your child essential Islamic supplications and the situations in which they would be used. Each book focuses on a single topic, with key vocabulary **highlighted**. These key words can then serve as a tool to remind your child of important points. All supplications are shown in Arabic text, translation, and transliteration. For any assertions regarding fiqh we have provided textual proofs, from the Qur'an and authentic Sunnah of the Prophet (saw), at the bottom of the relevant page. Each story is accompanied by original artwork, but in accordance with Islamic beliefs we do not use human or animal images.

Transliteration has been provided here as a means to help those who do not know Arabic to teach supplications to their children. But it must be noted that all transliteration is imperfect and cannot accurately represent Arabic sounds in their entirety. We therefore encourage anyone who uses our books to use the transliteration as a tool, but not an end in itself, and to eventually learn the supplications in the original Arabic.

In some cases, sounds will be represented in the transliteration (because they are present in the Arabic text) that will not actually be pronounced. These generally occur at the end of a supplication and are related to the Arabic rules for pausing and stopping. To clarify this for non-Arabic speakers, we have placed brackets [ ] around those sounds in the transliteration that would not be pronounced when reciting the supplication.

Thank you for purchasing this book, may Allah benefit both you and your child through it, forgive us for any errors we have made, and benefit us in this life and the Hereafter if there is any good in it.

Jameelah loved
Getting dressed every day,

She thought picking out clothes
Was a great way to play!

She liked digging through
Closets, drawers, and shelves…

She thought every child
Should try to dress themselves!

Jameelah looked in her closet,
(She always liked to start out there)

For the first thing she needed-
A pretty shirt she could wear.

She picked out a yellow one
Hanging up right in-between,

Two of her fancy dresses-
One orange and one green.

Now Jameelah had her shirt,
But she was not done...

She needed a skirt
For her getting dressed fun!

She looked and found one
That she really liked,

It was big and long,
And purple-green striped!

Next on her list…
A pair of socks for her feet.

They were in a high drawer,
Rolled up nice and neat.

To get to them,
Jameelah climbed up on a chair,

She considered a bit…
And then chose a red pair.

Hunting around for a Hijab,[1]
She looked in the top drawer…

It was last thing on her list
That she was looking for.

Jameelah reached right in,
And pulled out a few,

She thought for a minute-
Then decided on one that was blue!

---
[1] Head covering worn by Muslim women.

Jameelah got down
Off her chair with a hop,

Then went to her pile,
And put the last things on top.

She looked at her collection
Of clothes with pride,

Now all she had to do
Was get inside!

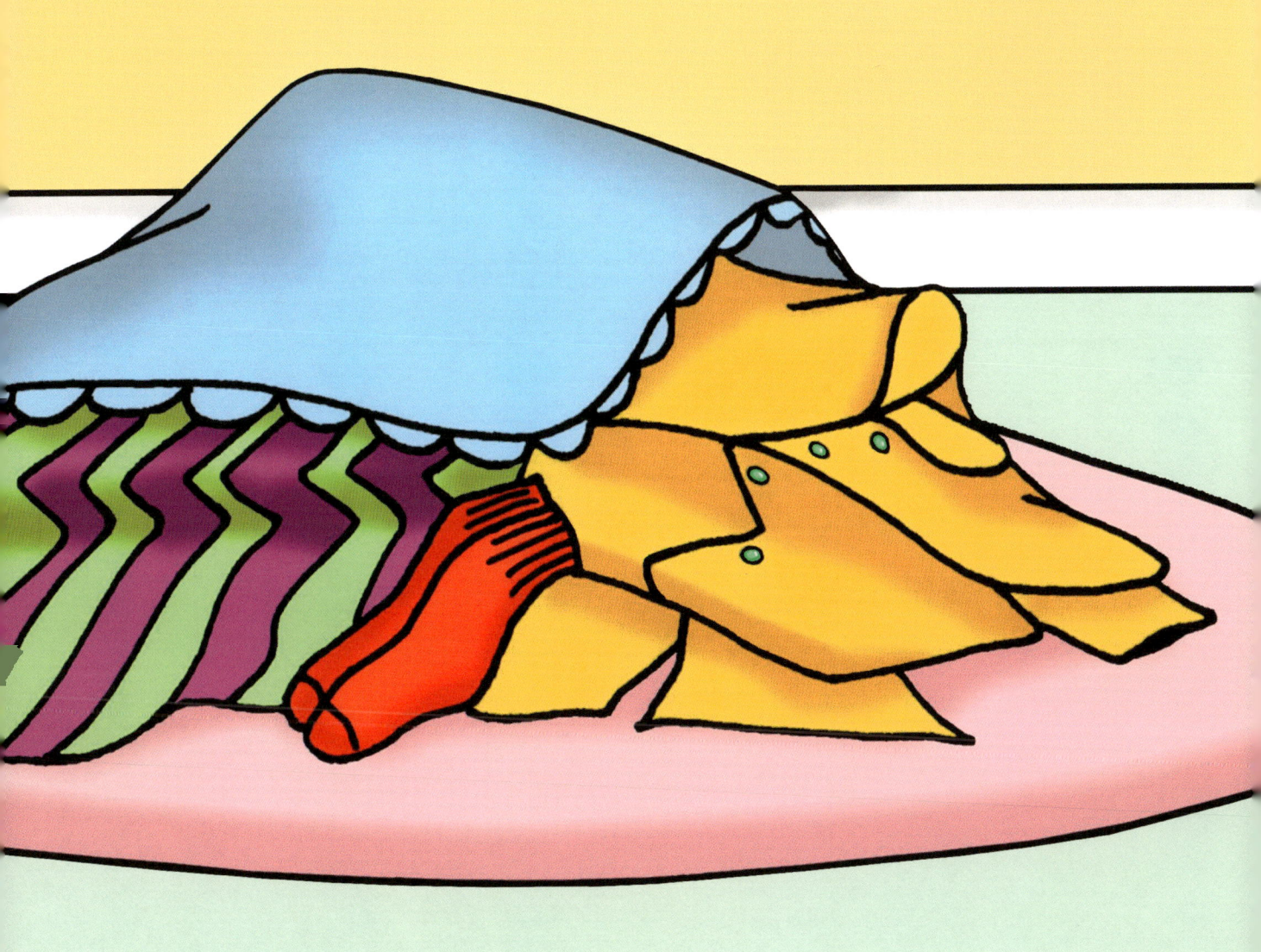

Starting with the shirt buttons,
She opened each one...

She loved to do buttons
They were so much fun!

When the last one was open,
She wiggled right in,

Then buttoned it carefully,
Back up to her chin.

Next, she carefully laid
Her skirt out on the bed,

Then she pulled it right up
And over the top of her head.

Then she tugged it down
Until it touched her toes,

A Muslim girl covers
As everyone knows![2]

---

[2] "O Prophet! Tell your wives and your daughters and the women of the believers to draw their cloaks all over their bodies." (Holy Qur'an 33:59)

Muslims like to start with the **right**[3]
In almost everything they do,

So, Jameelah started with her right
When she puts her socks on, too!

Then she looked in the mirror,
As she pinned her hijab-

Now her outfit was complete-
She thought she had done a great job!

---

[3] Aisha (raa) stated: "Allah's Messenger (saw) loved to begin with the right in all his matters, in putting on shoes, in combing his hair, and in purifying himself." (Muslim)

Then she said the special **du'a**
That we make when we are **dressing**,

Because Allah gives us clothing
As a very great **blessing**!4

اَلْحَمْدُ لِلَّهِ الَّذِي كَسَانِي هَذَا (الثَّوْبَ)

وَ رَزَقَنِيهِ مِنْ غَيْرِ حَوْلٍ مِنِّي وَ لاَ قُوَّةٍ

"Alhamdu lillaahil-lathee kasaanee hathaa (ath-thowba) wa razaqaneehi min ghayri howlim-minnee wa laa quwwa[tin]"

(All praise is for Allah who has clothed me with this garment and provided it for me, with no power nor might from myself5)

---

[4] "And Allah has made for you out of that which He has created shades, and has made for you places of refuge in the mountains, and has made for you garments to protect you from heat (and cold), and coats of mail to protect you from your (mutual) violence." (Holy Qur'an 16:81)

[5] Du'a Made When Getting Dressed (Al-Bukhaari, Muslim, Abu Dawud, At-Tirmidthi, and Ibn Maajah. See also: *Irwaa' al-Ghaleel* 7/47)

Then Jameelah thought
For a while about shoes,

Fuzzy pink slippers or green sandals-
Which one should she choose?

She decided on the slippers-
Because they were brand new!

They had come in a big blue box
With a fancy red ribbon, too!

She put her slippers on and stuck
Her fuzzy pink feet in the air,

Then said the **du'a** that we make
For **new things we wear**…

Du'a Made When Wearing Something New

اللَّهُمَّ لَكَ الْحَمْدُ أَنْتَ كَسَوْتَنِيهِ أَسْأَلُكَ مِنْ خَيْرِهِ وَ خَيْرِ مَا صُنِعَ لَهُ، وَ أَعُوذُ بِكَ مِنْ شَرِّهِ وَ شَرِّ مَا صُنِعَ لَهُ

"Allaahumma lakal-hamdu anta kasawtaneehi us-aluka min khayrihi wa khayri maa suni'a lah[u], wa a'oo-thu bika min sharrihi wa sharri maa suni'a lah[u]"

(O Allah, for You is all praise, You have clothed me with it [i.e. the garment] I ask You for the good of it and the good for which it was made, and I seek refuge with You from the evil of it and the evil for which it was made.[6])

---
[6] Abu Dawud, At-Tirmidthi. See also: Al-Albaani, *Mukhtasar Shamaa'il At-Tirmidthi*, pg.47

Just then, her mother came in
And sat down on the bed.

She saw Jameelah's new outfit,
Purple, green, yellow, blue, and red…

She saw Jameelah's fuzzy pink slippers,
Then looked at her and smiled,

"Jameelah," she said with a laugh,
"You're such a colorful child!"

"Do you know the du'a we say when **Someone else wears** something **new**?

You are wearing your **new** slippers
So, I'd like to teach it to you…"

تُبْلِي وَ يُخْلِفُ اللهُ تَعَالَى

"Tublee wa yukhliful-laahu ta'aalaa"

(May you wear it out and
Allah replace it with another.)[7]

---

[7] Du'a Made for Someone Wearing Something New (Abu Dawud 4/41. See also: Al-Albaani, *Sahih Sunan Abi Dawud* 2/760)

That night when Jameelah got ready
To go to bed and rest,

She made the **du'a** that we say
Before we get **undressed**…

"*Bismillaah*"

(In the name of Allah[8])

Each day Jameelah has lots of fun,
Picking out all kinds of clothes!

What will Jameelah wear tomorrow…
Only Allah (swt) knows!

---

[8] Du'a Made When Getting Undressed (At-Tirmidthi 2/505 and others. See also: *Irwaa' al-Ghaleel* #49 and *Sahihul-Jaami'* 3/203)

The End!

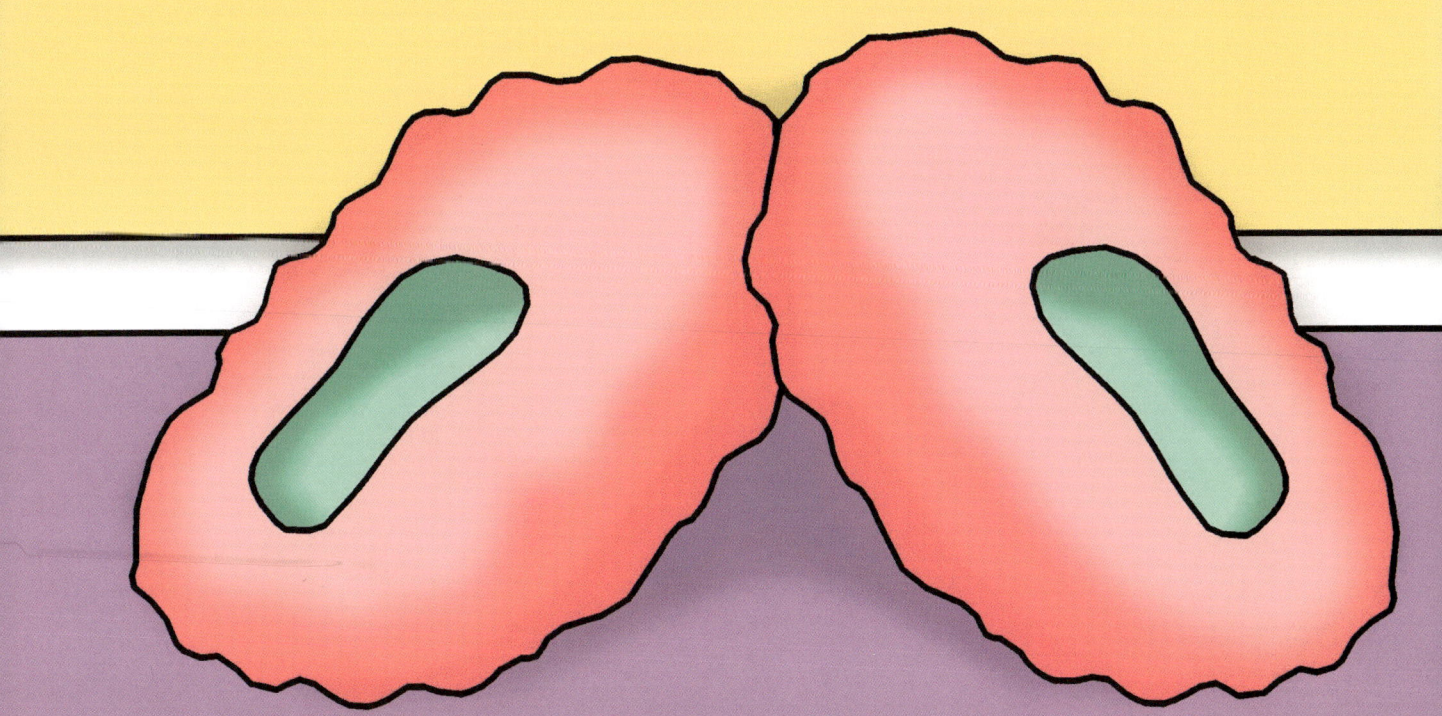

Other available titles in the Mini Mu'min Du'a Series:

Batool's Bedtime Story
Bilal's Bakery
Fatimah's First Fasting Day
Muhammed Goes to the Masjid
Sheema's Shopping Spree
Saliha Sneezes
Waheeda the Wudoo' Wonder
Waleed Wakes Up

and many more!...

Visit our online bookstore at:

www.Mini-Mumin.com

Made in the USA
Charleston, SC
13 January 2014